A sizzling delight of tantalizing tales that will keep you nibbling until you've cleaned your plate and are hungry for more. This collection of honest poetry describes the human experience of the crush/love/breakup cycle down to a tee. Nikki speaks directly to the Black Heart in all of us that 'quests' love, intimacy, and sex in all of its beautiful and warped tantalizing flavors. A must read for any lover of love. Where will Black Heart take us in Volume Two?

DJ
Author, Screenwriter, Podcaster, Reiki Master Teacher & Presenter.

Nikki's poems are real, raw, and vulnerable. In a world obsessed with perfection and highlight reels, we so desperately need that truth that Nikki gives us. Her poetry takes you on a ride through the human experience and truly makes you feel. Thank you, Nikki for sharing your heart with us!

MEGHAN SYLVESTER
Spirituality for Real Life. Kundalini, Creativity, Retreats

Reading Nikki's poems is like revisiting moments in your own life...from the depths of romantic despair to the joys, hopes, and yearning that envelope all human beings. The consistent message that is woven throughout is love, self-love, platonic love, romantic love, and the love of nature. And a wee bit of that whimsical fantasy too! I really admire the time she sets aside for the reader for personal reflection and meditation. Enjoy the journey of Black Heart Words & Poems.

CARRIE ROSSOW BOBERG
Filmmaker, Artist, and Friend

Published by Black Heart Alchemi
www.blackheartalchemi.com

United States of America

Cover design and graphics by David Rodriguez
Book layout and design by Nikki Rawnsley
Author Photograph by Fernando Viquez
Illustration for The Lion by Anomaly Arroyo

Black Heart Words & Poems:
An inspired anthology from the edge of darkness,
illuminated with a sprinkling of light /
by Nikki Rawnsley. – 1st edition.
1. Poetry
ISBN 9781959368007

Black Heart Words & Poems

Volume One

An inspired anthology from
the edge of darkness,
illuminated with a sprinkling of light.

Nikki Rawnsley

ISBN: 9781959368007

Dedication

These words have been written from my heart to yours.

I dedicate this anthology to all those who love a little too much and feel a little too deeply.

You deserve the best. You are not alone, and you are not lost.

I intend to inspire and awaken you. I hope that you will open up to your feelings. I encourage you to not suppress blocked emotions, but instead, as they come up embrace them and reflect on where they are rooted.

My desire is to crack open wounds from past hurts to let in the light and love of the universe.

Contents

Hi Lovers,

Meet the Author

Before we dive in; meet **Nikki Rawnsley**

Hello. My name is **Nikki Rawnsley**. I am the author of **Black Heart Words & Poems,** an anthology series inspired by my personal experiences: from the edge of darkness illuminated with a sprinkling of light.

My experience and background have always revolved around writing. I am a corporate professional; and a marketing business leader – so I write for a living.

I am a lover of words and the magic that words can communicate.

These poems are drawn from deep within me. My goal is to transcend and radiate the energy around me. With this prose I want to unleash the words to tease your mind, draw you in - and then crack open your heart.

Let me tell you a little bit more about this book:

Black Heart Words & Poems is an inspired anthology series inspired from the edge of darkness illuminated with a sprinkling of light.

I do include in a little of my whimsical side, it comes naturally.

When you read the poems, your own experiences will come to light, and it may elicit your own deep emotions.

We all bring our unique life experiences to what we read: love, heartbreak, pleasure, pain. These words may resonate, catapulting your own feelings to the surface.

Today, it is still almost frowned upon to show our vulnerabilities or to demonstrate any pain or grief.

But only by going through this journey, can you open up to true healing.

I have been on my personal healing journey for many, many years. As I opened up to my energetic healing it allowed me to tap into the profound inspiration to express my feelings, which is a healing in itself.

I want to share these poems with you. My intention is to make you feel alive deep within your core.

"I restore myself when I am alone"

– Marilyn Monroe

Introduction ♡
& Inspiration

Introduction and Inspiration

Thank you. Thank you. Thank you.

Thank you to those who inspired me to write these words.

You challenged me. You changed me. My life has been richer for it. I love you.

Not only did I write these poems for my self-love and healing, but also for those who have yearned for love, for those that have loved too deeply – and for those who have experienced unrequited love.

The words stem from the inspiration from my own life experiences as well as tales shared with me.

My goal is to tantalize you with this prose to elicit your own emotions.

Thank you to the many that read my first poems and responded by giving your heartfelt feedback.

I am grateful. I am blessed to have you in my life.

For those who are experiencing my words for the first time, I hope that you are inspired and that you feel a sense of community. My desire is that you are moved — and that you don't feel alone on your journey.

My intention is that you feel a deeper connection and compassion for all people on this planet.

When your heart feels heavy and dark, strive to live in the vibration of love and rejoice in the miracles around you.

Part One

Love is a Bitch

1

....

DRAW ME IN

DRAW ME IN

A moth to a flame.
You draw me in with your energy.
Our late-night talks and promises of light that are yet
to materialize.
I am addicted. Addicted to the unknown.
The sweetness of secrets and wishes yet to be
tasted keep me hungry.
I am a bat flying in the dark.
Unnourished and searching. Searching in the night.
Always the night.
I crave the beauty of the day but refuse to open my
eyes in case I get burned.

2

RECIPROCATE

RECIPROCATE

Trust me, I trust you.
See me, I watch you.
Listen to me, I hear you.
Feel me, I vibe you.
Want me, I desire you.
Respect me, I respect you.
Value me, I know your worth.
Appreciate me, I want you.
Love me, I will protect your heart.

♥

3

LOST

LOST
Your pretty eyes smiled at me, and you drew me in.
Your flirty words promised excitement and passion
and lit a fire.
Your wicked smile sent a warning to my unprotected
heart,
And I was lost.

♥

4

··

WHISPERS

WHISPERS

I whispered to the wind.
Sweetheart where are you?
The wind responded:
I am here, I've always been here.
But I can't see you.
Close your eyes to see better.
But I can't feel you.
Breathe deep and long. Can you feel me now?
Yes.
But I can't hear you.
Put your hand on your heart.
Do you hear me now?
Yes.

♥

5

SECRETS

SECRETS
Unspoken secrets at the edge of knowing.
Promises to understand.
But can you? Can you truly understand, or can you
only perceive from where you stand?
Stand.
Stand still. Feel. Hear. See.
Do you now know?
The secrets at the edge of knowing.

6

PATIENCE

PATIENCE
We seek out connections to feel whole.
But my dear, you are perfect the way you are, holes
and all.
The holes in you, are pieces of you that you gave to
others.
Sometimes willingly, which will be returned 10-fold.
Sometimes unwillingly. Stolen precious pieces that
leave a gaping gap to be replaced for something
better and more glorious.
Be patient and kind to yourself and even more to
those you encounter.
My dear, you never know how many holes they may
have.

7

MISSING YOU

MISSING YOU
How can you miss someone you've never met?
How can the distance between you cause a deep sad
empty feeling in your chest?
How can the longing and desire almost bring you to
tears?
My dear, energy is strong.
Energy is real.
But you too are strong.
 Stand up tall.
 Breathe deep.
 Straighten your wings.
 Open your heart.
The light shines on you.
Even when darkness drapes her veil across you,
know that it is temporary.
And only a test.
You will elevate higher. You are strong.

8

TRANSFORMATION

TRANSFORMATION
Walking slowly in the dark, heavily cloaked.
Shuffling along.
Looking down and not seeing.
Aimlessly moving without direction.
Quiet like a shadow.

Boom. Crack.
The thunder smacks with ferocity.
Crackle.
The lightening streaks across the sky.

You pull the collar higher around your neck, yet do not
hasten your pace.
Unmoved by the threat.
You aimlessly continue.
The clouds begin to retreat letting a sliver of light
penetrate through illuminating what looks like a path.

The booms of thunder have retreated and give way to
sounds of excited birds.
There is more light now, and the path is clear.
The warmth of the sun forces you to discard your coat
and you look up.

As you do your heart opens and you can see for the
first time.
You see the beauty all around.
The flowers, the stones on the path, the water on the
lake.

You are moved by this beauty, and you have transformed.

9

ENERGY

ENERGY

Is it possible to miss what was never there?
Yes.
It is not the actual thing that you miss.
But the possibilities and dreams it inspired.
It is the loss of those that you mourn.

But I feel sad and empty.
Of course, you do.
You created a vibration. An energy.
We are all energy my dear.
You gave that energy birth and named it, and it has
now left a hole.
That's why you perceive this emptiness.
Do not feel sad. Release it.
Let it go. With freedom it can grow.
Then another energy right for you will return and fill
the void with so much happiness and joy that you will
forget what you missed.

♥

10

TELL ME

TELL ME
Tell me about the weather and
I will tell you about the stars and the moon.
Show me the rain that falls from the sky.
I will tell the grass to grow and the flowers to
bloom.
Share about the storms that loom by with a feeling
of dread.
And I will cast a spell to keep us safe.
Describe the warmth of the sun on your back and
how it radiates brilliance all around.
I will use the shadows to create a dance to
celebrate life.

11

DARLING

DARLING

Darling, the words you crave to hear, say them to yourself.
You deserve to hear them. Say them often.

The love you desire to feel, give to yourself freely.
You are worthy.
Put on your best dress, kick up your heels.
Drink a glass of champagne like it's New Year's Eve.
It is a new day. Be a new you.
Dance. Sing. Celebrate.
Dance with the music turned up loud and with abandon.
Sing with energy and freedom.
Celebrate every day.
This day was created for you.
Darling, embrace it.

12

NAKED

NAKED
Are you naked?
Yes. I am vulnerable, uncovered. I am shy.
Don't be shy.
But what if you see 'ME'?

I have flaws and cracks. Scars from experiences in my past that run very deep.
I look strong on my exterior, but I am extremely fragile.

I may not respond well to your approach.
I might snap or bite from fear.
I may lash out and hurt you to protect myself.
I may dig my nails into your flesh, so you feel what I feel.
Are you naked?

♥

13

ON MY WAY

ON MY WAY
Hi, how are you?
I will be out of town for a while….
It's now the last week until I finish my project and
then we will connect…
I am sure…
Then next month I will come and visit you…
One more day and I'm done…
This week I will drive to see you, but it is far, 3-
days/28-hour journey…
Tomorrow for sure we will meet…
We will say "hi" at least…
In 10- or 11-hours' time I will be there. I will see
you…
…
… …
It's not looking good. Traffic is bad.
Appointments await…
I won't make it today…
I will call you tonight…
We will connect…
I am sure…
…
Goodnight

14

SELF LOVE

SELF LOVE
I love you.
She said to herself.
Then act like it.
  Stand Tall
  Breathe deep.
  Be Brave.
I don't know if I can.
You will for sure…
  Rise
  Inspire
  Elevate
How?
Don't worry. Just do it.

15

SOLITUDE

SOLITUDE
I am broken. I am chipped.
My flaws may not be that obvious.
Some days it takes everything to hold it together, and
not fall apart.
I wear the mask of a warrior.
I keep a sword by my side ready to slice and cut all
that come too close and threaten my solitude.
Being alone is my shield.

16

COME INSIDE

COME INSIDE
He came to feed off my light.
I was shining my brightest today.
He stared and then flinched but was unable to look away.
I cracked the door ajar and motioned him to come inside.
He was hesitant, but suddenly took three big steps then pushed the door wide as if knowing it would not stay open for long.
Long enough to enter. Long enough to come inside.
Long enough to feed off my light.

17

STALKERS

STALKERS
Tonight, I wanted to go out for a walk in the dark,
But not alone.
So, I tied on my shoes,
Threw on my jacket,
And grabbed my favorite murder podcast.
I stepped out into the night. I began my walk…
I walked down the road and around the block.
I held my head high and
tried to avoid the dog walkers and stalkers.

18

....

HEARTS DESIRE

HEARTS DESIRE
Pick a card the gypsy said.
I was nervous, my heart full of dread.
       Should I, Shan't I, will I pick a card?
       Or should I walk away?
Hold my head high and stay on guard.

Come here my dear, nothing to fear.
Your hearts desires I will foretell.
I am not a witch casting a spell.
Should I, Shan't I, will I pick a card?
       Or should I walk away?
Hold my head high or provide my soul to sell.

19

PULLED UNDER

PULLED UNDER
I am struggling not to be pulled under.
I try to retreat and run away, but it's no use.
A wave crashes down and drags me back.
    I gasp for air, then I am pulled under again.
    It is dark all around.
I try to reach the surface.
I need to breathe.
It's no use. I am dragged under again to the dark.
No more struggling.

20

QUESTIONS

QUESTIONS
Questions and answers
Run through my brain
Day and night
Fueling the flame
Fire crackling
Fire sparking
Fire burning in the night
Logic out the window
But out I step into the rain
Questions but still no answers run through my brain

21

IF ONLY

IF ONLY
If only we could be alone together
Together hidden from the world
Worlds apart from the reality outside
Outside where its cold and harsh

Harsh words from your lips
Lips that used to say words of love
Love so sweet and innocent, pure and light
Light no longer, only shadows exist

Existing on the memories of you
You, alone, without me
Me, alone without you
You and never we
We are alone and not together
If only we could be alone together

22

CONTROL

CONTROL
Losing control, but not wanting to let go
I don't want to get attached
But I feel like I already am
You are in my head and in my mind
When I am awake, I see you
When I am asleep, I dream of you
When I am away from you, I feel you

♥

23

HOLDING ON

HOLDING ON
Holding on too tight
But afraid to let go
Mind racing
Can't sleep
Call to the moon
Reach for the stars
Ask the universe to answer my prayers
Holding on too tight
Afraid to stay
What would that do to me
Should I venture that way
Mind out of control
Thoughts dancing
Constant waking
Sun searing
Wind bustling
Breathe out. Release
The universe silently obeys

♥

24

BE MINE

BE MINE
Be here
Be present
Be kind
Be patient
Be mine

Believe
Behave
Be real
Be mine

Be there
Be on time
Bewitched
Be mine

25

RETREAT

RETREAT
She retreats into the woods with her crystals and incense.
To the magic of nature to soothe and heal her wounded soul.

Her only witnesses are the animals and birds, the moon, and the stars.

They howl and flutter as she gives herself over to let the healing begin.

....

STRONG

STRONG
Don't be sad
Be focused and strong
Be patient
Pause. Regroup. Reflect.
Be brave.
You can do it.
It might take some time.
Breathe. Be more patient.
You've got this.
I know you can do it.
You are strong

27

....

DARK BELOW

DARK BELOW

Stay away was the warning in my head flashing like a neon sign.

Be quiet as a mouse.

Don't get caught in that tangled web.

Hide in the dark. Crouch down.

Don't be seen.

Shhhhhhhhhhhhhh

That was the beginning of the end.

The end of light and descent into darkness.

Deep into the caves below that held all the secrets.

28

TAKE ME TO BED

TAKE ME TO BED
Take me to bed
Nighttime is a sensual time
The world outside has retreated within
Make yourself a cup of tea, or pour a glass of wine
& take me to bed
Get really comfortable and relaxed
In our special place
Take me to bed

I don't care what you look like
You could be ragged around the edges
Your face all worn
That's OK. It is likely you have more truth to share
Take me to bed

Your words are like magic
They turn me on
Take me to bed

I can't keep my eyes opens
But I don't want the story to end
Put in a bookmark or fold down the page corner
Place me on the nightstand. Goodnight
Tomorrow, we begin another chapter
Take me to bed

1000 PIECES

1000 PIECES
My heart is broken into a thousand sharp pieces.

When I try to breathe, I feel the shards tearing and
ripping at me from within.
It is racing so fast I can hear it in my head,
pounding away so loudly.

Make it stop I yell.
Give me some peace.

It is relentless that pounding noise. The searing pain.

Yelling at me that it was all my fault.
My fault for not protecting my heart.
My fault for being too careless trying to allow love in.

Only to have it smashed into a thousand pieces.

30

DIFFERENT WORLDS

DIFFERENT WORLDS
We are from different worlds.
Our language is not the same.
You are beautiful. I am plain.
I like chocolate. You like vanilla.
I am not from here and you know all the roads.
I don't have a compass to know where to go.
You are running and I am standing still.
You are the recent future, and I am the near past.
Like a magnet I feel the pull.
Then in an instant it is flipped, and I am repelled,
pushed with such a force I cry out.
The longer I stand still the further apart we are.
I am left longing for the memory of your touch.
X

31

PLAY

PLAY
Come out and play.
You said it would be fun.
No one will get hurt, it's just fun.
Let's play hide and seek you say.
You hide and I will come and find you.
I will count to twenty.
Hide well.
Hide very well.
She was never seen again.

♥

32

....

ROCK

ROCK
Today I felt like crying.
The emotion was so raw and intense. It feels like it
will wash over me and drown me.
I don't know why.
Life is grand, beautiful, glorious.
But I feel so sad.
The heaviness is pulling at me evermore.
I struggle to push it away and it surrounds me
instead like a sticky grey cloud.

Get off. Go away I scream.
But there is no sound.
I struggle in vain but to no avail.
I am trapped here for what feels like an eternity or
longer.

Why can no one see this or hear my screams.
I am here. Help me.
Nothingness. Greyness. It is all around.
Once where I saw color and joy it is just a dirty
grey smudge.
Where I used to hear the birds singing, I now hear
hollow echoes.
The world continues, it flows as if I am not here.
I sit trapped. I wait motionless.
I am just a rock.

33

TEARS

TEARS

Instead of crying tears, the words poured onto the page.
Like tears from the clouds.
It was as if my heart had been cracked open and all the stored emotions escaped like demonic beings spreading across the pages.
They showed no desire to stop and stay.
They kept flowing out without boundaries.
Cementing the pain that was unleashed with them.
When you try to hold onto something too tight.
You will be torn up, shredded, mangled, bloodied, beaten, and dragged as if caught in a tornado.
Only to be spat out down the road when the storm dies down.

34

BLACK HEART

BLACK HEART
She wore her heart on her sleeve like a badge
of honor.
All who looked could see the scars.
Her heart was black and bruised yet still
managed
to beat.
A deep dark heartbeat.

·····································

SCRITCH SCRATCH

SCRITCH SCRATCH

I love writing. Writing on paper.
That feel of the pen gliding across pristine white paper.
Now the page is streaked with blemishes.
Thoughts streaming from my brain, my heart, my pain, my past, my future, my wishes, and desires.
Dripping my document with fear, with hopes, anticipation, and experiences.
As if manifesting it to the universe. Calling to it with fresh ink.

I love the sound that writing makes. When you dot the i and cross the t.
The staccato of this movement is like music. The sound of the mechanics the pen makes moving as the magic of the words spill onto the page.

I love to scratch out something I no longer want to say with a harsh scritch scratch.
Then it is obliterated. If it were only that simple to abolish all things, especially those deep, deep feelings.
Those pesky feelings you can't keep at bay.
You can't just scritch scratch them away.
They will return with vengeance no matter how hard you try to suppress them.

You can begin to rewrite how you react to take out the sting they bring.

So, grab your pen and begin again.
It may begin messy or fantastical.

Write your life.
Scritch Scratch out the things you don't want and edit your best life along the way.

It does not have to be beautiful prose just so long as it flows and gives your emotions a place to land.

It is safer and healthier that they take root on the page and not locked up deep within.

Once these words have escaped your mind and fallen on the page leave it to the mighty unseen powers to work their magic and take away their power.

Scritch Scratch.
Grab a new page and start again.

Your Turn

Your Turn

Take a moment to reflect on a love that moved you.

It need not be romantic. It could be that of a child, a friend, a sister, a brother, or beloved cat or dog.
It need not to be an actual love, but that feeling that you felt in the center of your chest.

- Grab a favorite pen or pencil.
- A big notebook or blank paper to write on. You could even use your phone or laptop.
- Find a quiet area.

MEDITATE

Before you begin take a moment to get centered. Remove all distractions. Turn off your phone and go to an area where you will not be disturbed.
Choose a favorite meditation to allow you to tap into your heart center and begin.

Let your words just flow. Do not try to stop and correct them. You can do that after when you re-read it and take time to reflect on it.

_____

_____

_____

_____

_____

_____

_____

_____

_____

_____

_____

_____

Part Two - Wild Beasts

36

....

THE HUMMINGBIRD AND
THE LIZARD

**THE HUMMINGBIRD AND
THE LIZARD**

As I sat in my yard, I noticed a tiny lizard.
The ones you often see that keep quiet while
eating bugs.
He was small. Maybe only a baby.
Running out from the protection of the bushes to a
patch of tall grass, he bobbed and swayed and
danced in the sun.

Overhead circled a black bird. Did he see the
lizard from so far away?

Just a moment later a beautiful hummingbird appeared from nowhere.
He began fluttering above the lizard as if communicating the imminent danger.

The black bird continued to circle as the hummingbird flapped its wings and the lizard danced in the sun.

The hummingbird descended lower closer to the lizard urging it to retreat into the bushes.
As if heading the flurried call, the lizard ran into hiding.
The black bird circled again and then flew away.

The hummingbird stayed around the bushes as if to say it's safe you can come out now.
And just like that the lizard reappeared.
He ran to the grass and danced in the sun as his tiny protector buzzed close overhead.

It has been a month since I witnessed this friendship in the garden.
The lizard is still there but much larger now.
He often startles me by running up a wall or rustling through the bushes.
He is brave and rules the ground.
His friend the hummingbird is never too far protecting from the air.

THE SCORPION

THE SCORPION
I was warned. Don't get too close.
Do not reach out your hand for fear of getting hurt.

I am brave. This creature is beautiful.
He won't attack me.
His head nodded in agreement while he held his tail
with stinger high.

But in a flash.
I got stung by the scorpion.
It hurt so deep.
As the tears ran down my cheeks
The poison slowly flowed deep in my heart.
I knew it was killing me inside, but I stood tall and hid
the pain.
I did not stand a chance.

♥

38

....

THE TALE

THE TALE
Come into my web said the spider to the fly.
I have a tale to tell.
The fly approached close to listen
That was the end of the fly.

♥

39

THE LION

THE LION
You terrify me. I said to the lion.
No need to be afraid. Come closer. Warm yourself
against my coat.

I am a bit cold. Just for a moment then.
I approached with trepidation. Tip toeing closer to
this majestic beast.

As I approached, I could hear his breath. I could
see the saliva dripping from his jowls like he was
salivating.
Come closer he breathed. You are cold, I will
protect you.

Like a mouse I moved a little closer.
He did not move. Just kept his gaze fixated on me.
I stepped around his gigantic paws, reflecting that
with just one swipe and I would be gone.
He still did not move except for his large tail
flicking back and forth.

Come closer. You are shivering.
I was, but not from cold. I was shaking down to my
core.

I will keep you warm, the Lion said, with a voice so
deep and smooth.

I was so close now that I could feel his breath.

So close that I could feel the moisture within it.
I was so close that I could stare into his eyes and
see a glint of what looked like hunger.

Come closer. I won't bite.

I was too close now that I could not run.
I touched his fur. It was silky soft and so warm.
I wanted so much to melt into it.

You can touch it. Come closer he breathed again.

I was now inches from him.
Patiently he again assured me that I would be ok.

I broke from his gaze and in one swipe, one bite
he devoured me.
The saliva swung from him and dripped from his
mouth, and I was gone.

40

THE FAIRY

THE FAIRY
You ripped off my wings and I was forced to walk on the ground.
No longer able to float like I used to.
As I stepped my feet throbbed.
The place where my wings used to be ached.
My head dropped as I looked down instead of up.
I embraced the dark.
Stumbling into the night.
Where only demons thrive.

41

RECIPE

RECIPE
A pinch of pepper and a dash of salt.
Two frogs' legs and eye of newt.
Stir them together and sing a song.
Under the full moon of spring.
Wish, then await your fate.

42

NIGHT

NIGHT
It is nighttime again.
My favorite time of the day.
The time when nothing good comes out to play.

It comes out cloaked in dark to dance with the moon
and the stars.
The howls in the distance of crickets nearby create a
nighttime concert only a few souls will hear.

And then too soon the sun breaks the first light, the
night sounds are gone.
The creatures vanish with the threat of day.
The stars fade and the moon retreats.
And the birds come out to sing their songs.

I drudge through the day to wait for the night, my
favorite time of day.

Your Turn

Your Turn

Take a moment to get grounded. Try to be in nature.

If you can't put your feet or butt on the ground, just look out of the window or sit near a house plant.

Look at the relationships in nature and write about these.

Your favorite pet? Think about the birds you see. Really look closely, like you have not ever done before.

Tap into that feeling deep in your heart.

- Grab a favorite pen or pencil.
- A big notebook or blank paper to write on. You could even use your phone or laptop.
- Find a quiet area.

MEDITATE

Before you begin take a moment to get centered. Remove all distractions.

Turn off your phone and go to an area where you will not be disturbed.

Choose a favorite meditation to allow you to tap into your heart center and begin.

Let your words just flow. Do not try to stop and correct them. You can do that after when you re-read it and take time to reflect on it.

Acknowledgments

Acknowledgments

Many people have helped bring this book to life and for this I am forever grateful, no matter what role you played. You may not even know the impact that you have had on my creative journey.

Some people broke my heart, some who left me wondering; and then there were a few who were just not at the same place at the same time that I was to commit to the love I was looking for. I am thankful that our lives crossed and for the lessons and the inspiration that led me to find the words that now fill these pages.

To my friends and family that have always encouraged me to pursue my goals and dreams, thank you! I am blessed beyond words for your support. To brave friends that openly shared your dark moments, your experiences, and stories and allowed me to draw on these. Thank you. I offer you healing and a voice.

Thank you to my mum who provided proofreading, support, and high fives along the way.

To my spiritual communities that provided me with meditations and tools to stay grounded, connected, and inspired during both the tough times as well as those times of euphoria. This has been invaluable. Sat Nam.

To my writing mentors and coaches past and present. You have paved the way by providing a path to follow. The power of your words inspires me.

A huge thank you especially to Tuesday May Thomas (DJ), an inspirational author, teacher, guide, and friend. You can't choose your family, but often a family bond finds you outside of bloodlines and this is a rare and beautiful gift. Learn more about DJ at www.holisticmysticpodcast.com

To Meg Sylvester a beautiful, enlightened sister who openly wears her heart on her sleeve providing a safe place for grounding and connection. I am thankful that our paths crossed. I am inspired every day by your words and actions.
Instagram: @meghansylvester
www.megsylvester.com

To Carrie Rossow Boberg, a former colleague, fellow creative force, a beautiful well-rounded soul, and lover of words, thank you for your friendship, support, and inspiration.

To David Rodriguez, thank you for your beautiful design support. Your work is not only always stunning, but your authentic support of my project is so very appreciated. Follow on Instagram @davidisraelrg

To Anomaly Arroyo, thank you for your beautiful drawing of The Lion to add drama to one of my favorite poems. And for supporting my creative journey through my words as you continue to pursue your creative talents as a visual artist, it means so much. Follow on Instagram @aaanomolyyy

I am grateful and privileged to have an outlet to transform emotions into prose and tales.

To you those of you who have picked up this book, I trust you gain as much enjoyment from reading it, as I did from creating it. I send you much love.

Only through experiences can we grow. We often grow the most when we have experienced pain and taken the time to reflect on it. When you choose to learn from these lessons you will grow to your highest self.

I am blessed in more ways than you can imagine. If you like these poems, please stay connected as Volume Two is already in the works.

Follow me on Instagram @BlackHeart_Alchemi or sign up for updates from www.blackheartalchemi.com.

Want More?

Want More?

 Follow on Instagram
@Blackheart_Alchemi

Fresh words, inspiration, community, and connection.

♥ Order a copy of the book for a friend or someone that illuminates your heart.

Black Heart Words & Poems

An inspired anthology from the edge of darkness, illuminated with a sprinkling of light.

♥ Support other writers. Read their words.

♥ Start your own writing practice.

♥ Visit www.BlackHeartAlchemi.com

Words are like magic, a powerful energy you can use to effect change around you. To craft your world into existence. Embrace these gifts.

Words carry potent magic. They evoke feelings, manifest healings. Words can connect or divide. They impact the way people find their place in the world.
Remember this and spell wisely.

About the Author

Nikki Rawnsley

She is a corporate professional, marketing business leader, a prolific writer, and author.

She has had the opportunity to travel extensively and meet people from all around the world. With her empathetic qualities and a natural curiosity, she feels deeply, and this is where she draws her inspiration for her poetry.

When tapping into her creativity she often turns to her whimsical side, diving deep within her soul where she is a winged fairy, a nymph of the woods or a ninja warrior -- ally for nature.

She is a spiritual seeker, high vibe living world traveler.
A British-born Australian residing in California. USA.
Her daily practice is to live in love for the highest good of all.

When writing, her goal is to transform and radiate energy around her. With words and prose, she will tease the mind, draw you in - and then crack open your heart.

Resources

Resources

These poems are intended to untangle the strings tied around your heart.
As you begin to remove them you may be triggered.
It is important that you always take care of yourself.
You are loved. You are worthy.

Here are some resources should you find yourself going a little too close to the edge.

USA

If you are in a life-threatening place, call 911.
You can also call or SMS 988, Suicide and Crisis Lifeline.
Or visit Mentalhealth.gov

Outside of the USA you can call:
Canada: 911
Mexico: 066 or 911
UK: 999 or 112
Ireland: 999 or 112
Netherlands: 112
Germany: 112
France: 112
Australia: 000 or 112
New Zealand: 111
South Africa: 112 on mobile devices.

Emergency help line in your location.

Made in the USA
Middletown, DE
21 October 2022

13094004R00046